IMAGES
of America

MOTORCYCLING IN CALIFORNIA'S CENTRAL VALLEY

ON THE COVER: Chas. C. Russell Harley-Davidson Motorcycles was at 531 East Market Street in Stockton (across from the modern *Record* building). In this 1911 photograph, nine just-uncrated Harley-Davidson model A motorcycles are lined up at the curb, with handlebars and seats not yet installed. The model A had a 30 cubic inch (ci) single-cylinder engine—the famous V-twin would be featured in 1912—and belt drive. Renault Grey was the only color, so Harleys were nicknamed "grey fellows." Owner Charles Cornelius Russell, 24, is at center wearing a vest. (Charlie Russell, Elaine Burke.)

IMAGES
of America

MOTORCYCLING IN CALIFORNIA'S CENTRAL VALLEY

Stewart Barber Sr. and David R. Stuart

ARCADIA
PUBLISHING

Copyright © 2023 by Stewart Barber Sr. and David R. Stuart
ISBN 978-1-4671-0891-1

Published by Arcadia Publishing
Charleston, South Carolina

Printed in the United States of America

Library of Congress Control Number: 2022947296

For all general information, please contact Arcadia Publishing:
Telephone 843-853-2070
Fax 843-853-0044
E-mail sales@arcadiapublishing.com
For customer service and orders:
Toll-Free 1-888-313-2665

Visit us on the Internet at www.arcadiapublishing.com

*Dedicated to Valley motorcyclists of yesterday, today, and tomorrow,
and to Art Stuart Sr. of Ripon, a San Joaquin County and
California Highway Patrol officer from 1927 to 1950.*

IMAGES
of America

MOTORCYCLING IN CALIFORNIA'S CENTRAL VALLEY

Stewart Barber Sr. and David R. Stuart

ARCADIA
PUBLISHING

Published by Arcadia Publishing
Charleston, South Carolina

Printed in the United States of America

Library of Congress Control Number: 2022947296

For all general information, please contact Arcadia Publishing:
Telephone 843-853-2070
Fax 843-853-0044
E-mail sales@arcadiapublishing.com
For customer service and orders:
Toll-Free 1-888-313-2665

Visit us on the Internet at www.arcadiapublishing.com

*Dedicated to Valley motorcyclists of yesterday, today, and tomorrow,
and to Art Stuart Sr. of Ripon, a San Joaquin County and
California Highway Patrol officer from 1927 to 1950.*

CONTENTS

ACKNOWLEDGMENTS

Thanks to all who allowed us to share your heritage through photographs and stories. Special thanks to the Sage family, David Kaften, the Harley-Davidson Archives, the American Motorcyclist Association Hall of Fame, and Tim Ulmer Photography. Unfortunately, not all contributed photographs could be included due to the publisher's image quality standards and page and layout limits. Photograph contributors are credited throughout with the following abbreviations:

AC	Alton Compasso		KS	Kevin Shawver
AJ	Alex Jorgensen		LH	Linda Haworth collection
AMA	American Motorcyclist Association Hall of Fame Museum		LMC	Lodi Motorcycle Club
			MB	Mike Buckenham collection
AM	ArchiveMoto.com		McG	McGill family collection
B	Dick and Delores Blank collection		MJ	Mike Johnston
BF	Brooking family		ML	Mike Law
BOS	Bank of Stockton Archives		MS	Michael Sanguinetti
BZ	Bozzie family		MV	Mark Vukovich
C	Coleman family collection		PL	Stockton–San Joaquin Public Library
CA	Carl Alvarez collection		PLC	Patty Lemon collection
CHP	California Highway Patrol		PMU	Police Motor Units LLC
CM	Chris Mazzanti collection		PSMC	Port Stockton Motorcycle Club
CPC	Chris and Pamela Carr		R	Rendon family collection
CR	Chris Ranuio		RC	Ron Chapman collection
CREB	Charlie Russell, Elaine Burke		RF	Reiman family collection
CSUS	California State University-Stanislaus		RH	Richard Hardmeyer collection
DK	David Kaften collection		RHS	Ripon Historical Society
DS	David Stuart		RL	Ralph Lee family collection
EL	Everett Lucas collection		RM	Ron Myer
FC	Frank Colli collection		RP	Roy Perez collection
GB	Graffigna Bros.		RS	Richard Schmidt collection
GG	Gary P. Garavaglia		RV	ridingvintage.com
GK	Gary Kinst collection		S	Sage family collection
GWMP	George A. Wyman Memorial Project		SBHS	San Benito County Historical Society
H	Hiles family collection		SF	Sikeotis family
HD	Harley-Davidson Archives		SJCHM	San Joaquin County Historical Museum
HF	Holland family		SK	Stephanie Kendall collection
HM	Haggin Museum		SMC	Stockton Motorcycle Club
J	Jorgensen family collection		SP	Sylvia Perez collection
JF	Jimmy Filice		SPD	Stockton Police Department
JJ	John Jessup collection		TH	Tom Howard collection
JO	Jimmy Odom		UOP	University of the Pacific, Holt-Atherton Special Collections
K	Kendall family collection		VB	Vickie Bradford Bell
KCD	Kathleen Casenave Dragovich		WSP	West Side Pioneers Association (Tracy)
KE	Kathleen Ehrhardt		YM	Yosemite Meat Market
KM	Ken Magri			

INTRODUCTION

Residents in the heart of the Central Valley—the northern San Joaquin Valley from Lodi, Stockton, Manteca, and Tracy in San Joaquin County, through Oakdale, Modesto, and Turlock in Stanislaus County—embraced motorcycling from the beginning of the sport and lifestyle. The region's mild Mediterranean climate, with the longest frost-free period in the Great Central Valley, provided ideal riding weather from March through November.

The favorable climate and the flat terrain were also ideal for bicycling, the forerunner of motorcycling. The Valley heartland was a leading participant in the bicycling craze at the end of the Victorian era. In the 1890s, three hundred American manufacturers were selling a total of more than a million bicycles each year. Every small town in the Valley had at least one bicycle club for men and women, especially after the development of the "safety bicycle," bikes with wheels the same size and a pedal crank driving the rear wheel. Recreational bicycling helped to free women from many past social limitations.

Bicycle racing was a popular spectator sport, and the first simple motorcycles—really motorized bicycles—were used as "windsplitters" to pace bicycle racers. Bicycle dealers and repair shops were plentiful and provided a ready-made sales, service, and support structure for the emerging motorcycle manufacturers.

Several British bicycle companies began making motorized bicycles, led by Excelsior in 1896 and including Royal Enfield (1901), Triumph (1902), and Norton (1902), followed by the Birmingham Small Arms Company (BSA) in 1910.

Motorcycle manufacturers were emerging in the United States, too. The Hendee/Indian Motocycle Manufacturing Company of Springfield, Massachusetts, was started in 1901 by a popular bicycle racer. Indian was the most successful brand before World War I, and by 1913 was producing more than 30,000 motorcycles per year. The iconic Harley-Davidson Motor Company of Milwaukee, Wisconsin, was established in 1903. Two years later, the Excelsior Motor Manufacturing & Supply Company of Chicago, Illinois, began production. Other early US motorcycle brands included Thor, Racycle, Cleveland, Pope, Yale, Henderson, Monarch, Pierce, Curtiss, Merkel, Sears, Miami, Reading-Standard, Wagner, Dayton, Flanders, Jefferson, Imperial, Ace, and Cyclone.

The northern San Joaquin Valley had a good supply of potential motorcycle riders and repairmen not only because of the popularity of bicycling, but also because it was a center for mechanical innovation and manufacturing. Agricultural machinery companies employed thousands of mechanical workers, best exemplified by the Holt Manufacturing Company of Stockton. Holt developed and produced innovative combined grain harvesters/threshers and Caterpillar tractors, both now recognized as world engineering landmarks. The Holt factory covered six square blocks and employed more than 2,500 workers.

"The Chicago of the West," Stockton in 1900 had about 300 foundries and manufacturing companies in addition to Holt, producing farm equipment, pumps, engines, food processing equipment, building materials, dredges, and boats and ships. Many years of strife between management and labor were easing, and industrial workers were getting more time off and seeking new leisure activities.

Agriculture in the Central Valley—the base of the economy since the 1860s—rapidly mechanized and most farmers were quick to appreciate new technology, including motorcycles. The number of farm families in Stanislaus and San Joaquin Counties grew rapidly in the 1910s, primarily because the creation of local irrigation districts allowed huge tracts of dry-farmed grain to be subdivided into many smaller farms. Motorcycles provided farmers with a convenient way to go into town.

City-to-city motorcycle endurance runs and lengthy races on tracks were popular in the earliest days of motorcycling. Endurance was taken to the extreme by Northern California bicyclist George Wyman, who was the first to ride a motorized vehicle, a motorcycle, from coast to coast in 1903 (see chapter six, page 116).

Spectator sports were significant pastimes before mass-media entertainment such as radio and television. The earliest motorcycle races in front of large crowds were at banked wooden ("board") bicycle velodromes, renamed "motordromes" and "speedways." College stadiums and horse tracks were repurposed as unpaved ("dirt") motorcycle flat tracks.

Clever motorsports promoters created exciting competitions and spectacles, including team events and relays. In 1912, for example, the First on the Coast Team Competition at Agricultural Park in Sacramento pitted motorcycle riders from Stockton against the capital city's finest racers. Motorcycle manufacturers sponsored professional racing teams, and popular early "factory riders" included Lathrop's Otto Walker and Oakdale's Albert "Shrimp" Burns (see chapter six, pages 117 and 118).

World War I, The Great War in Europe (1914–1918), was the first mechanized global conflict in which warring nations used airplanes, submarines, and tanks—the latter based on Stockton's Caterpillar tractor. Motorcycle racing was put on hold, but motorcycles were used by the militaries, particularly for reconnaissance and delivering messages. The 1915 Triumph model H, called "the Trusty" and considered by many to be the first modern motorcycle, was developed for use by Allied forces and propelled the British company to become a major global brand.

To meet the motorcycle needs of US doughboys overseas, the federal government contracted with the three largest American manufacturers. Excelsior received a contract for 3,500 motorcycles, primarily used in the Italian Alps, but the Chicago company struggled to compete with the other two contractors, Indian and Harley-Davidson.

Indian was the leading American manufacturer at the time and was initially contracted for 20,000 of its rugged Powerplus V-twins and later for an additional 20,000—essentially its total output. The scale of that production challenge and a zero, or even negative, profit margin left Indian a weakened company after the war.

Harley-Davidson received government contracts for a total of about 18,000 V-twin motorcycles, a bit more than a third of its total production. Harley was able to continue developing its products during the war, including overhead valve engines, giving it a leg up in the post-war marketplace. Harley became the best-selling brand in post–World War I America.

Many of the men returning after World War I became motorcycle enthusiasts in the 1920s, purchasing Harleys, Indians, Excelsiors, and other brands. The Stockton Motorcycle Club first appeared in the newspapers in January 1914, publicizing road rides to Mount Hamilton above San Jose in February and to Lake Tahoe on Independence Day. The club was put on hold during the war and was formally re-established in 1924 after the Spanish flu pandemic had subsided.

Spectator sports such as boxing, college football, baseball, horse racing, and motorcycle racing remained popular in the roaring 1920s. Motorcycle hill climber Dudley Perkins, who began his career in Stockton, was among the era's most popular motorsports champions (see chapter six, page 119).

Military use and racing contributed to improved mechanical reliability, and motorcycles were applied to uses other than personal transportation and recreation. The Stockton Police Department (PD) had added a motorcycle officer in 1912, one of the first in California and America. Other northern San Joaquin Valley PDs were also early to use motorcycles—the Modesto PD, for example, had a full, organized motorcycle unit in 1921.

Roads throughout the Central Valley were patrolled by city and county motorcycle officers, and in 1920, Fresno motorcycle officers started the San Joaquin Valley Traffic Officers Association. The organization was renamed the California Association of Highway Patrolmen in 1921 and it continued after the state created the California Highway Patrol in 1929.

Motorcycle officer Lavon B. New of the Turlock PD was the first Stanislaus County peace officer to die in the line of duty. He died in August 1935 following an accident in June during a pursuit on Highway 99 at Geer Road.

Automobiles became abundant and accessible with Ford's ground-breaking Model T. By 1928, President Hoover would promise "a car in every garage," and by the end of the decade, four out of five families owned one. The Golden State Highway through the Central Valley, now known as Highway 99, was one of the first highways in California; it was begun in 1915 and was paved in the early 1920s. The transcontinental Lincoln Highway also passed through in the 1920s, connecting Sacramento, through Lodi, Stockton, and Tracy, over Altamont Pass to the East Bay, and via ferry to San Francisco.

The regional population grew and suburbs like Tuxedo Park in northwest Stockton were increasingly dependent on personal transportation, as were commercial strips that culminated in Stockton's Miracle Mile and Modesto's suburban McHenry Village in the early 1950s. Many consumers purchased affordable cars rather than less-practical motorcycles. Harley-Davidson showed its marketing savvy by promoting supplementary merchandise eliciting the motorcycling lifestyle and sense of community.

Industry boomed in the 1920s, technology advanced, motorcycle design improved, and production increased. Then the Great Depression, triggered by the stock market crash of 1929, rang the death knell for most motorcycle brands. By 1931, only Harley-Davidson and Indian survived as American motorcycle manufacturers and their rivalry remained preeminent until Indian ceased production in 1956. Motorcycle races provided affordable entertainment in the 1930s, and racers such as Leonard Andres had devoted fan bases (see chapter six, page 120).

During World War II (1939–1945), Harley-Davidson stopped civilian sales after it obtained exclusive federal contracts to supply motorcycles and training for the US armed forces. More than 85,000 Harleys were used during World War II.

The war effort brought tens of thousands of soldiers, sailors, and civilian workers to the northern San Joaquin Valley, which was strategically distant from seaborne attacks but was served by the inland Port of Stockton and multiple railroads and highways. Military facilities in the heart of the Valley included Ballico Auxiliary Airfield and the Army Rehabilitation Center in Turlock, Hammond Hospital (the largest military hospital on the west coast) and Modesto Auxiliary Airfield in Modesto, the Riverbank aircraft aluminum and ammunitions plant, Sharpe Depot in Lathrop, Tracy Depot and New Jerusalem Auxiliary Airfield in Tracy, Kingsbury (now Kingdon) Auxiliary Airfield near Lodi, and Stockton Army Airfield, Stockton Ordnance Depot, and the Rough and Ready Island Naval Supply Annex in Stockton. Shipyards on the Stockton Deep Water Channel employed 10,000 civilian workers. Valley farmers and canneries went into overdrive to feed American soldiers and sailors.

The Port Stockton Motorcycle Club was formed by workers at the Naval Supply Annex in 1937—it was first called the Vagabonds but was renamed 10 years later when it acquired a clubhouse. The Modesto Motorcycle Club was established in 1939. In about 1940, the Port Stockton club became one of the first clubs sanctioned by the American Motorcyclist Association (AMA) to admit women as full members.

The postwar era brought unprecedented prosperity and a growing blue-collar middle class to the heart of the Valley, in stark contrast with the decade prior to the war. In the late 1940s and the 1950s, former sailors and soldiers settled into civilian family life. Many chose inexpensive military surplus Harleys and recreational motorcycling to continue the camaraderie they had enjoyed during the war.

Veterans of the European campaigns had been introduced to Triumphs and other brands overseas, which created interest in lighter motorcycles and contributed to the stripped-down "bobber" trend. Dealers such as Leonard Andres (Modesto and Stockton) and Glen McGill (Stockton and Lodi) provided motorcyclists with services, support, and equipment.

"Rosie the Riveters" had acquired much independence during World War II and sought their own freedoms and recreational expressions, with or without men. The Lodi Comets all-women motorcycle club thrived in the 1950s, and its first president became a national spokesperson. The Tracy Gear Jammers auxiliary was one of two females-only clubs to attend the infamous 1947 Independence Day weekend gathering in Hollister. That AMA-sanctioned Gypsy Tour event was crashed by a hundred non-affiliated troublemakers and was sensationalized by a pair of San Francisco reporters and *Look* magazine. The reporting spawned *The Wild One* movie in 1953 and fueled the outlaw biker mystique.

The heart of the Central Valley was ideal for motorcycle road rides to locations that continue to be tourist destinations: the San Francisco Bay Area, coastal redwood forests, and Pacific beach towns such as Santa Cruz and Dillon Beach; Lake Tahoe, Calaveras Big Trees, Yosemite, and dozens of lakes and reservoirs in the forests of the central Sierra Nevada; the quaint gold rush towns along Highway 49 in the Sierra foothills gold country; the state capital region; and the unique Sacramento–San Joaquin Delta and beautiful orchards and vineyards of the Great Central Valley.

These places were the settings for club picnics and field meets, which brought clubs together and featured good-natured competition in fun events such as slow races, balloon busts, poker runs, plank jumps, scavenger hunts, trials maneuvers, blindfold rides, potato pickup races, and motorcycle polo.

Postwar racing venues included William Micke's oak grove (now a regional park between Stockton and Lodi), Baxter Stadium at College of the Pacific, Lodi Stadium (the Grape Bowl), 99 Stadium (Stockton 99 Speedway), the track at Modesto Junior College, and horse tracks including the one at the San Joaquin County Fairgrounds. AMA Grand National series races at flat oval dirt tracks—short track, half-mile, mile, and TT events—blossomed after the war and remain very popular. In the early 1950s, airports such as New Jerusalem near Tracy and Kingdon near Lodi started to be used for drag racing.

Lodi Cycle Bowl was developed by the Lodi Motorcycle Club beginning in 1953, using a borrow pit excavated during the construction of Highway 99. The quarter-mile short track/TT venue was a learning track for newcomers including Modesto's Kenny Roberts Sr. and Stockton's Alex Jorgensen, Chris Carr, and Fred Merkel, all of whom are now AMA Hall of Fame honorees (see chapter six, pages 122–124, 126).

Motorcycle road racing gained popularity in the 1950s. Stockton native Brad Andres dominated paved road courses, setting the stage for future international Grand Prix Road Racing stars including Roberts, Merkel, and Modesto's Jimmy Filice (see chapter six, pages 121 and 125).

British motorcycle brands including Triumph, Norton, and BSA gave increasing competition to the American icon Harley-Davidson in the 1950s. In the mid-1960s, Japanese-made motorcycles became predominant—brands such as Yamaha, Suzuki, Kawasaki, and Honda. The availability and affordability of these brands extended the reach of motorcycling deep into the Boomer generation.

Off-road vehicle recreation areas were developed by California State Parks in the coastal range hills above Tracy and in the Sierra Nevada foothills near Folsom and Rancho Cordova (Sacramento County). Stanislaus County developed off-road riding areas near La Grange (30 miles east of Modesto) and in the hills 25 miles west of Patterson. These public venues—which had been used by heartland off-road riders and hill climbers since the 1920s—supported off-road riding and motocross, enduro, hill climb, and scrambles races.

The photographs in this book illustrate the love of motorcycling in the northern San Joaquin Valley, from the first motorized bicycles in the early 1900s through spirited racing competition in the 1960s. Vintage pictures commemorate the AMA Hall of Famers and the dealers, mechanics, and riders who made contributions to the sport, lifestyle, and community. Proud working riders such as police officers and soldiers are depicted too, as are several of the clubs that brought heartland motorcyclists together over the decades. Enjoy the ride!

One

Shops, Dealers, Mechanics, and Speed Tuners

Members of the Oakleaf Wheelmen bicycle club are shown parading their safety bicycles on Stockton's Weber Avenue in 1895. Bicycling was extremely popular in the 1890s and 1900s; it was the forerunner to motorcycling in the 1910s. Central Valley towns had active bicycle clubs and many bicycle shops. For example, in 1910, Lodi had a population of fewer than 2,700 people, yet it had four bicycle shops: two on School Street and one each on Main and Sacramento Streets. The first motorcycles were sold and serviced in the 1910s by existing local bicycle shops such as these. (HM.)

The Graffigna Bros. Excelsior Auto Cycle (motorcycle) dealership was at 108 North Sacramento Street in Lodi (now Graffigna Bros. Auto Parts). In this photograph from 1911, an early motorcycle is being wheeled onto the sales floor among many bicycles. (BOS.)

Graffigna Bros. repairmen are shown working on a Flanders model 4 motorcycle in the repair shop. Flanders motorcycles were made in Chelsea, Michigan, from 1911–1913. They had four-stroke, single-cylinder engines that produced four horsepower, hence the model designation. (GB.)

Oakdale Cyclery, "Motor Cycle Headquarters," was at 125 North Third Street (now Oak Valley Community Bank). The shop and 17 bicyclists are seen in this photograph from about 1910. (BOS.)

Land & Dorr Bicycles, Motorcycles, and Sundries was at 430-432 Weber Avenue in Stockton (near the current Children's Museum). Here, in 1911, a Thor motorcycle is at center, flanked by Indian motorcycles. Repairman Dudley Perkins, second from left, started racing in the Central Valley and went on to become a National Hill Climb champion and a Harley-Davidson dealer. The AMA's most prestigious award is named after him (see pages 88, 89, and 119). (S.)

This photograph shows the Land & Dorr sales room on Weber Avenue in 1911. Co-owner William A. Dorr is standing second from left; co-owner Chester A. Land is on the right. (S.)

Shown in the Land & Dorr repair shop are, from left to right, owners William A. Dorr and Chester A. Land with an unidentified worker. An Indian motorcycle is in the foreground. (S.)

14

Chas. C. Russell Harley-Davidson Motorcycles was at 531 East Market Street in Stockton (across from the modern *Record* building). In this 1911 photograph, nine just-uncrated Harley-Davidson model A motorcycles are lined up at the curb. Owner Charles Cornelius Russell, 24, is at center wearing a vest. (CREB.)

Brady's Cyclery, a Thor and Pierce motorcycle dealership at 44 South California Street in Stockton, is shown in 1913. Thor was the brand produced by the Aurora (Illinois) Automatic Machinery Company, which in the early 1900s made engines for Indian and many other brands. The Pierce Company of Buffalo, New York, is better remembered for Pierce-Arrow automobiles, but it also made innovative motorcycles from 1909 to 1914. (S.)

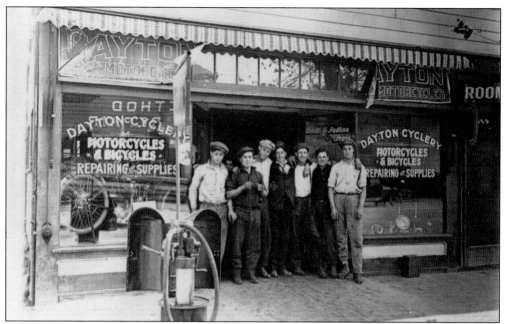

Joseph Gotelli and Modesto Padlina owned Dayton Cyclery at 228 South Center Street in Stockton. Dayton motorcycles were made from 1914 to 1918 by the Davis Sewing Machine Company of Dayton, Ohio. On the far right in this 1915 photograph is Angelo Rolleri, one of the founders of the beloved Genova Bakery. (BOS.)

The Stockton Motorcycle and Supply Company, an Indian dealership, occupied the same building as the prior Land & Dorr shop (see pages 13 and 14). This photograph was taken after a rare Stockton snowfall in 1914. By 1913, Indian had become the largest motorcycle manufacturer in the world, producing more than 30,000 units per year. The 1914 model featured a 61ci V-twin engine, chain drive, and a single-speed transmission with hand and foot clutches. (S.)

Pictured on the sales floor of the Graffigna Bros. shop in Lodi is a new 1915 Harley-Davidson V-twin model J with electric lights and the pedals not yet attached (this was the last year with starter pedals). A 1915 Miami Power Bicycle, a small single-cylinder motorcycle, is in the foreground, made by the Miami (Ohio) Cycle Manufacturing Company. (GB.)

Turlock's Snider's Cyclery, a Thor dealership, is shown around 1920. Sixteen riders are pictured astride Thor (right), Indian, and other motorcycles in front of the shop. The Snider family opened its first bicycle shop in Bakersfield (Kern County) in 1904, and started selling motorcycles shortly thereafter. (CSUS.)

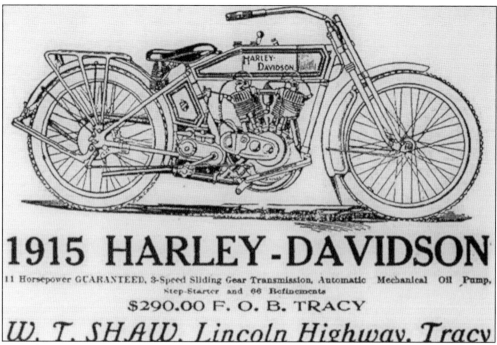

1915 HARLEY-DAVIDSON

11 Horsepower GUARANTEED, 3-Speed Sliding Gear Transmission, Automatic Mechanical Oil Pump, Step-Starter and 66 Refinements

$290.00 F. O. B. TRACY

W. T. SHAW, Lincoln Highway, Tracy

W.T. Shaw's Motorcycle Hospital, an Indian and Harley-Davidson dealership, was open 24 hours and was strategically located on the Lincoln Highway in Tracy. The Lincoln Highway was the first transcontinental highway; in 1913–1927, it went through Sacramento, Lodi, Stockton, and Tracy, then over Altamont Pass to the Berkeley Pier ferry, connecting to San Francisco. (PL.)

The Stockton Motorcycle Supply Company (see page 16) assembled an effective display at the 1916 auto show, showcasing new Indian Powerplus V-twin motorcycles. (S.)

Mechanics James "Red" Craig (left) and Joe Simpson were caught taking a break in 1950. Red was a tuner for dirt track racers Lammy Lamoreaux and Shorty Thompson in the 1930s–1940s. Famed New Zealand tuner/racer Burt Munro came to Stockton in the 1960s to consult with Red, preparing the "world's fastest Indian" for record runs at Bonneville. Simpson worked at Joe Vitone's shop in Stockton. (MB.)

Joe Vitone owned the Stockton Cycle Company, a dealer for English BSA, AJS, Matchless, and HRD motorcycles and Italian Lambretta scooters. The shop was at 1100 East Main Street in Stockton. (RL.)

The Leonard Andres Harley-Davidson dealership was at 1208 Ninth Street in Modesto, as shown here in about 1950. Andres also bought "Soapy" Sudmeier's Harley dealership at 729 North Wilson Way in Stockton and later opened a dealership in San Diego (see page 120). (Above, RL; below, CR.)

Gene Andres is shown at the counter of Leonard Andres Harley-Davidson in Modesto in 1953. (RL.)

Chet Hanchett was a mechanic for Leonard Andres Harley-Davidson in Modesto. He is pictured in the repair shop in 1953. (RL.)

Bus Schaller, a speed tuner from Turlock, is shown working on a Harley-Davidson WR in 1953. (RL.)

Melvin "Red" Fenwick was the other renowned speed tuner nicknamed Red. In this photograph from 1953, he is working in the repair shop of a Modesto BSA dealership. (RL.)

McGill's Indian Motorcycles, also called Lodi Cyclery, was at 312 South Central Avenue in Lodi (now adjacent to Torres Appliances). In this 1950 photograph, mechanic Jack Cottrell poses on an Indian motorcycle in front of the shop. (McG.)

Service with a smile! From left to right, Glen, Johnny, and Dolly McGill are shown at the counter of their motorcycle shop in Stockton in about 1952 (see page 25). (McG.)

Frank Burke owned the BSA, Triumph, and Mustang dealership at 1410 Ninth Street, Modesto, in the early 1950s. Mustang was a lightweight motorcycle made in Glendale (Los Angeles County) from 1946 to 1965. English motorcycles such as Triumph and BSA were then competing strongly with American brands. (RL.)

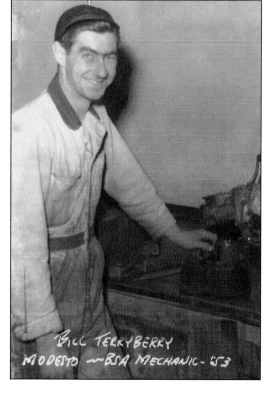

Bill Terryberry was a mechanic in Frank Burke's shop. He was a close friend of Bud Aksland from Manteca (see page 114) and a speed tuner for Grand National Championship Series Harley-Davidson racing bikes. Like so many mechanics, he was a master craftsman and an unsung hero of the motorcycling community. (RL.)

Glen A. McGill Motorcycles was at 1850 Cherokee Lane/Road in Stockton. This early 1960s photograph shows customers (from left to right) Jake Hayre, Karl Ross, Ira Shaw, Frasier McGill, Frank and Barbara Tendel, unidentified, Tom Howard, Don Stover, Delwin Archer, Warren Blackburn, Archie Clark, Mike Buckenham, Len Allen, and unidentified. (McG.)

From left to right, Al Williams, Tom Howard, and an unidentified mechanic pose in front of the Motorcycle Center at 1812 Harding Way in Stockton (now D&S Motoworks) in about 1960. The onslaught of Japanese-made motorcycles, hinted at in this storefront and display, would characterize the remainder of the decade. (TH.)

1965 Davis Bros. Harley Davidson shop
Donates a Harley Davidson MC to benefit the
Stockton Police Drum & Drill Assoc.(SPYA)
Stockton Commodores Drum & Bugle Corps Archives-Roy Perez

Davis Bros. Harley Davidson, 729 North Wilson Way in Stockton (previously Leonard Andrus Harley-Davidson, now H&R Block), donated an Italian-made 50 cubic centimeter (cc) Harley-Davidson M50 Sport Cycle motorbike to benefit the Stockton Police Department's Commodores Drum and Bugle Corps in 1965. This photograph in front of the shop shows, from left to right, the Davis brothers, officer Ethel Alvarez, and officer Delores "Dee" Blank. (RP.)

Three legendary Harley-Davidson dealers were photographed on historic motorcycles in 1976. From left to right are Leonard Andres (Modesto, Stockton, San Diego), Armando Magri (Sacramento), and Gene Andres (Modesto, Stockton, San Diego). Magri was on Harley-Davidson's oldest preserved motorcycle. (KM.)

Two

MOTORCYCLISTS IN THE HEART OF THE CENTRAL VALLEY

In this 1913 photograph, a rider sits on a Thor motorcycle in front of the first Southern Pacific Railroad depot in Stockton (replaced in 1930 by the second SP Depot, a block east at 949 East Channel Street). The image evokes both the transition from railroads to highways and the emergence of personal mechanical transportation. Motorcycles had evolved from the first motorized bicycles introduced 10 years earlier; by the mid-1910s, they provided reasonable personal transportation, competitive in both cost and reliability with horseback, horse-drawn buggy, and the automobiles of the time. (BOS.)

In 1912, a rider on an Excelsior motorcycle was photographed riding eastbound on Tracy's Eleventh Street (now Interstate Highway 205 Business). (GK.)

Hazel and Leslie Von Dack of Tracy seemed proud of Les's new 1913 Harley-Davidson V-twin. Rudolph and Zoe Patzer Von Dack, Les's parents, are in the background at their home on East Tenth Street. (WSP.)

Claude Rice of Stockton poses with his 1914 Thor V-twin and his canine companion. The dog's name is not known, but he was a good boy. Rice was a glass blower married to Catherine Welser. They lived on American Street and raised three sons in Stockton. (K.)

This heavily accessorized 1913 Indian V-twin and its unidentified owner were photographed in about 1914, before laws required headlights and horns. (RL.)

Claude Clifford and Alice Perry of Lockeford (San Joaquin County) are on a rare 1911 Excelsior Auto Cycle V-twin in this photograph from about 1912. The Excelsior company was purchased in 1912 by bicycle magnate Ignaz Schwinn and became the third-largest motorcycle manufacturer in the United States. (SJCHM.)

Robert Franklin Rush of Stockton is shown sitting on a 1914 Yale V-twin motorcycle. The Yale brand, made in Toledo, Ohio, was at its peak and winning many board-track races in 1914, but production ceased the following year. In 1906, Yale acquired the rights to the design of the California-brand motorcycle on which George Wyman had made the first transcontinental ride (see page 116). (PCL.)

William Lee Bryant of Stockton was photographed in 1916 riding his 1914 Excelsior motorcycle. (LH.)

Bryant and his wife, Ivie Marie (McKasson), posed later that year with their toddler son Henry Leon. William and Ivie eventually had nine children. (LH.)

Louisa Maria Basso and Attilio Luigi Salini of Stockton are pictured on a 1916 Indian Powerplus V-twin. He immigrated from Italy to Stockton and worked at a cannery as a loader. She worked at the same cannery as a fruit cutter. They married, had three children, and lived on Sierra Nevada Street. (KCD.)

This photograph from about 1918 shows Thomas Virgil Schmidt of Stockton on his 1915 Indian Powerplus V-twin. "Virg" was vice president of Graven Inglis Bakery. (RS).

At least two members of Ripon's First Christian Reformed Church rode their motorcycles to services—a 1913 V-twin Indian (left) and a 1916–1917 Excelsior. The church was built in 1917 by the Society for the Promotion of the Spiritual Welfare of Hollanders at Ripon. When Ripon incorporated in 1945, the building was the first city hall. It is now the Veteran's Memorial Museum. (RHS.)

John Greer, standing at right, poses with his sisters, niece, and brother Charles on his Harley-Davidson model J in about 1920. One can imagine Charles telling the rural San Joaquin County residents how handy the motorcycle was for running into town for supplies or to attend church. (SJCHM.)

This 1916–1921 model J Harley-Davidson motorcycle was the pride and joy of these patriotic Stocktonians. (SMC.)

Victor Wiles of rural Stockton and an unidentified woman pose with his 1921 Harley-Davidson 74ci model JD. (DK.)

Robert Franklin Rush of Stockton is pictured on an Indian motorcycle with a sidecar in the mid-1920s. A decade earlier, Rush was a winning motorcycle racer (see pages 30 and 85). In 1919, he was a motorcycle mechanic at Liberty Cyclery, and in 1920, at Hansel and Ortman of Stockton. (PLC.)

Albert Jr. and Dolly Compasso of Stockton pose on his 1936 Harley-Davidson OHV EL, with Albert Compasso Sr. (standing), in 1938. Albert Jr. was a member of the Vagabonds Motorcycle Club of Stockton. So was Leonard Andres, who worked at Soapy Sudmeier's Harley shop and really wanted this bike. Times were hard, so Albert Jr. sold it to him a year later when Dolly was expecting son Gary. (AC.)

Motorcycles provided economical transportation and recreation during the Great Depression in the 1930s. Lodians Alice and Walter Werner (left) on an Indian motorcycle are pictured with Betty and Roger Janzen in this photograph from about 1939. (LMC.)

This 1940s photograph shows Roger and Gertrude Nicholson of Stockton on a new Indian Chief at Lake Tahoe. Roger was a Marine veteran of Iwo Jima and a life member of the Stockton Motorcycle Club (see chapter four). (SMC.)

Frank Colli Sr. of Tracy is shown in 1945 on a 1939 Indian with a "watermelon stripe" tank; it reached 108 miles per hour in a quarter-mile drag race. Colli was a president of the Tracy Gear Jammers Motorcycle Club (see chapter four), a Golden Gloves boxer, and a cattleman. (FC.)

Vernon Meade of Lodi poses on his new Indian inline four motorcycle in 1940. Indian produced models with inline four-cylinder engines from 1927 through 1942 (see page 52). (LMC.)

Alice Werner of Lodi is shown in the early 1940s on an Indian motorcycle at Ospital Canyon (now called Hospital Creek). The location was a popular hill-climbing locale in the Diablo Range hills of southwest San Joaquin County (see page 92). (SJCHM.)

Frasier McGill sits on his Indian Chief in his Stockton yard in about 1946. (McG.)

Alex Ranuio (right) and friends pose on 1941–1946 Harley-Davidsons before a ride in the mid-1940s. (CR.)

Ruby Alvarez of Stockton is shown starting her 1949 Indian Scout, with daughter Barbara. (CA.)

Emil Croce was one of many Stocktonians who rode surplus World War II military edition Harley-Davidsons after the war. He was the owner of the Avenue Inn and was proud of its back bar, which was shipped to California around Cape Horn. (SMC.)

Edith Ehrhardt rides an Indian Scout on Lockeford Street, Lodi, in about 1950. She was the first president of the all-women Lodi Comets Motorcycle Club (see chapter four). (LMC.)

Myron "Mike" Lubin (left) and August "Sharkey" Alvarez of Stockton pose on their 1948 and 1951 Harley-Davidsons. (CA.)

Beulah Stover of Stockton (left) and Edith Ehrhardt of Lodi are shown in about 1952. (LMC.)

Edith Ehrhardt was photographed in 1954 with the AMA's Most Popular and Typical Girl Rider trophy. Ehrhardt sits on a new Harley-Davidson KH in Leonard Andres's salesroom in Stockton. (LMC.)

Edith Erhardt was a national spokesperson and advertising model. She toured the country, sponsored by AMA and corporate sponsors such as Duckworth motorcycle chains, and promoted women's involvement in motorcycling. She visited motorcycle clubs (see page 80), dealers, and major races, including the Daytona 200 in Florida. (McG.)

Cuffed jeans, white tees, and leather jackets were not the only "uniforms" worn by mid-1950s motorcyclists. In September 1956, Paul Autieri of San Francisco was judged Best Dressed Rider in the Lodi Grape Festival/National Wine Show parade. (RL.)

Many motorcyclists customized their "rides" to express their personality and creativity. This 1949 or 1950 Harley-Davidson "panhead" is a good example, with many added lights and decorative elements. (RL.)

Mike Buckenham, holding his brother John Willie, poses with his 1948 Ariel 500cc Red Hunter on Golden Gate Avenue in Stockton. He owned Buckenham's Stuttgart West shop for European automobiles. (MB.)

Beulah Stover was photographed on a BSA motorcycle in 1955. Nimble British motorcycles were popular with women riders, competing with the products of the main American manufacturers, rivals Harley-Davidson and Indian. (LMC.)

On the left in this photograph is a 1924 Harley-Davidson model JC ridden in a parade on Lodi's Church Street in the mid-1950s. (S.)

John "Natso" Villiborghi of Stockton is shown at a field meet in 1955. He was called "Natso" for often saying, "That is not so!" Natso was a charter member of the Stockton Motorcycle Club (see page 61). (SMC.)

This photograph from about 1958 shows, from front to back, Kim, Alex, and John Jorgensen of Stockton. Father "Jorgy" (John) was a motorcycle dealer in Stockton and a racer. Son "Jorgy" (Alex) became a Hall of Fame racer (see page 122). Kim became an excellent racer, too. (J.)

Dick Blank of Stockton poses on his 500cc AJS motorcycle (Albert J. Stevens Company from England) in the early 1960s. Blank was president of the Port Stockton Motorcycle Club (see chapter four). (B.)

Delores "Dee" Blank of Stockton was a Stockton Police Department motorcycle officer for 30 years (see pages 26 and 58) and a firing range master instructor. She is shown with a Harley-Davidson XLH in about 1961. (B.)

Dee and Dick Blank of Stockton were both life members of the Port Stockton Motorcycle Club and owned the Cycle Haven motorcycle shop at 1405 East Miner Avenue in Stockton. (B.)

This March 1966 photograph was taken in front of the Beta Theta Pi house at the University of the Pacific in Stockton. The motorcycle is a Honda CL77, 305cc Scrambler. Scramblers were dual-purpose bikes with some off-road capability—having higher exhaust systems, skid plates, and beefier tires. It was a cool ride for "Joe College" in the era of Japanese-made motorcycles. (BOS.)

Tom Howard of Stockton was an actor and a stuntman for the popular *Hardy Boys* television series. This 1967 photograph shows Howard (left) with lead actor Parker Stevenson. (TH.)

Three

MOTOR OFFICERS, SOLDIERS, AND DELIVERERS

The first mechanized global war, World War I (1914–1918), featured Stockton's Holt Caterpillar tractors to pull artillery and as the basis for tanks. Motorcycles were vital communications and scouting vehicles. In this postwar photograph, the US Army 143rd Field Artillery Regiment, Battery C displays at the Stockton Armory some of the equipment used during the Great War in Europe. Shown are Model 1897 guns and limbers used until 1933; Caterpillar Twenty and Thirty tractors; 1921–1924 Harley-Davidson model J or JD motorcycles with sidecars; and in the background on the right, the Armory, built in 1930 at 1420 North California Street. (UOP.)

Stockton PD traffic officers H.A. DuBois (left) and J. Philo Shoemaker pose astride Indian Scout motorcycles in 1923 in front of the Western Pacific Railroad depot, which was built in 1908 at 1025 East Main Street (near Union Street). The Stockton PD used a motorcycle before World War I, in 1912, and after the war had one of the first traffic units in the Central Valley. These officers may have belonged to the San Joaquin Valley Traffic Officers Association, established in 1920. (BOS.)

This photograph at the same location shows members of the San Joaquin County Traffic Squad in 1925. County officers patrolled the non-municipal roads in the county and were members of the California Association of Highway Patrolmen prior to the 1929 establishment of the California Highway Patrol. The second officer from the left is Leland Drais; the others are unidentified. (SJCHM.)

The Yosemite Meat Market at 915 North Yosemite Street in Stockton used a Harley-Davidson JD with a sidecar to make deliveries. This photograph is from 1929. The meat market/deli is still in business. (YM.)

In 1929, the Stockton PD parking patrol used a Harley-Davidson JD with a sidecar. (BOS.)

California Highway Patrol motorcycle officers pose in front of the Stockton Memorial Civic Auditorium at 525 North Center Street in 1930. Art Stuart Sr. of Ripon, grandfather of author David Stuart, is third from right; George Baron is fourth from right with an inline four-cylinder Indian. The other motorcycles are Harley-Davidsons and the other officers are unidentified. (DS.)

Sgt. George Baron, a California Highway Patrol officer, is shown in 1931. Baron patrolled from Tracy to Livermore on an Indian inline four motorcycle. Indian got the inline design when it acquired the Ace Motor Company in 1927; this is the Indian model 402 with a sturdier frame, introduced in 1929. (RC.)

The delivery motorcycle used by Stockton's Reiman Photo Service in the late 1930s was a Harley-Davidson 45ci model RL, the popularity of which helped Harley survive the Great Depression. (MJ.)

Harley-Davidson motorcycles (1932–1933 model VLs) and patrol cars are displayed by California Highway Patrol officers in the mid-1930s in front of the Stockton Memorial Civic Auditorium. Sgt. Art Stuart of Ripon is standing in the back row on the right; the others are unidentified. (DS.)

This late 1930s photograph shows Doug McCaullay of Stockton with a modified Harley-Davidson VL used by the US Army. When the United States later entered World War II, Harley was contracted to produce tens of thousands of special military model motorcycles (see page 56). (DK.)

California Highway Patrol motor officers from the Stockton office were photographed in 1939. Sergeant Baron is fourth from left; the other officers are unidentified. (RC).

Stockton PD officer George Brooks is shown on a Harley-Davidson motorcycle in about 1940. A native of Stockton, Brooks served 35 years starting in 1939, with 10 years on motorcycle patrol. (CM.)

Officer Brooks is making a traffic stop in this 1942 photograph. Patrolling on a motorcycle in winter was tough—notice the grill cover on the automobile to prevent radiator freezing, Brooks's leather jacket, and the fabric fairing and windshield added to the motorcycle. Perhaps this is why Brooks never owned his own personal motorcycle. (CM.)

Sgt. Loren R. McCrimmon of Stockton served in New Guinea. McCrimmon is shown in 1942 on a Harley-Davidson 45ci "small twin" WLA (US Army model based on the WL civilian model), nicknamed "the Liberator." More than 85,000 Harley motorcycles were used in World War II. (MV).

California Highway Patrol officer Glen Blackburn worked with the motorcycle safety program in the early 1950s, during the postwar boom in motorcycling. CHP motor officers established relationships with motorcycle clubs focused on improving safety (see page 68). (RL.)

The classical 1926 Stockton City Hall, at 425 North El Dorado Street, provided the backdrop for this photograph of Stockton Police Department assets, including, from left to right, a three-wheeled Harley-Davidson Servi-Car, a Harley-Davidson motorcycle, and five 1958 Plymouth Belvedere patrol cars. (BOS.)

Barbara Waltz was the first female motor officer with the Stockton Police Department (see page 59). She is pictured around 1957 in front of Davis Bros. Harley-Davidson. (BOS.)

Stockton PD parking officers in 1959 included, from left to right, Ethel Alvarez, Loraine Catelli, and Barbara (Waltz) Hardin. They used three-wheeled Harley-Davidson Servi-Cars. (BOS.)

Stockton PD officer Delores "Dee" Blank of Stockton (see pages 26 and 47) was photographed in 1959 doing parking patrol on a Harley-Davidson Servi-Car. (SPD.)

This photograph from Barbara Waltz's scrapbook shows Stockton Police Department officers Barbara "Big Red" Waltz (left) and Loraine "Cat" Catelli leading the Stockton–San Joaquin County Chambers of Commerce float in the 1957 San Francisco Lions Club Convention Parade. Police motorcycle escorts, including Harley-Davidson Servi-Cars such as these, were a symbol of respect and prestige. Waltz wrote in her scrapbook that she "stalled that three-legged beast in front of the Judge's Stand!" (BOS.)

Stockton Police Department motorcycle officers pose in front of city hall on El Dorado Street. From left to right are Anton Hinrichson, Fred Kurth, Al Garavaglia, Bill Rodinsky, Rick Scott, Don Garibaldi, John Penero, Ray Brudesnich, Charlie Buck, Rich Cordova, and Frank Drendoll. (GG.)

This Stockton PD motorcycle officer was photographed "in pursuit" in 1967. (SPD.)

Four

Motorcycle Club Members

The Stockton Motorcycle Club was active by January 1914, when it publicized road rides to Mount Hamilton above San Jose in February and to Lake Tahoe on the Fourth of July. The club was suspended during World War I but was re-established in 1924 after the troops had returned from Europe and the fourth wave of the Spanish influenza pandemic had passed. This photograph taken by John Stagnaro shows, at far left, Peter Bayer Sr., known by club members as "Mr. Bayer" (in whose machine shop the club met) and 1924 charter members, from left to right, John Villiborghi, George Chappuis, Pete Bayer, an unidentified onlooker, Ed Jones, Humphry Jones, Jake Bayer, Joe Croce, John Croce, and Andy Garibaldi. Chappuis was a machinist from Lodi, John Croce and Garibaldi were farmers, and the others worked for Sterling Pumps. (SMC.)

Members and friends of the Stockton Motorcycle Club pose for a late 1920s group photograph in their clubhouse at Bayer's machine shop at Polk and Mariposa Streets. (DK.)

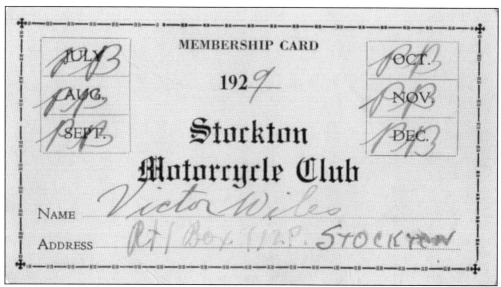

This is the membership card of Victor Wiles. He lived in the rural Waterloo area east of Stockton, near highway 88, and although he was not a charter member of the Stockton Motorcycle Club, he was a motorcyclist in the early 1920s (see page 34) and a member by 1929. In World War II, Wiles served in the US Army Air Corps and because of his motorcycling experience was tasked with adapting military motorcycles (see page 56) for use on snow—a project that was not successful. (DK.)

Repairs often had to be made on the roadside. The unidentified club members shown here are working on a 1925 Harley-Davidson JD; the other motorcycle (left) is a 1930 Harley-Davidson VL. (DK.)

This late 1920s photograph is of Stockton Motorcycle Club members preparing for a road ride. (DK.)

"Mt. Hamilton or Bust?" is painted on the sidecar on the left, giving the destination of the Stockton Motorcycle Club members assembled for a road ride in about 1930. The ride to Mount Hamilton, the site of the Lick Observatory, was 80 miles through beautiful Del Puerto Canyon, east of Patterson in Stanislaus County. (DK.)

Gypsy Tours were large gatherings of AMA-affiliated clubs from throughout a region. This photograph is of the AMA District 36 or Valley Council gathering at Sonora, Tuolumne County, in 1939. (RH.)

The 1939 Lodi Motorcycle Club motorcycle polo team poses before its match in Jackson (Amador County) against the Three Point Motorcycle Club from Hollywood. From left to right are Walt Werner, Dave Buckmiller, Ezra Ehrhardt, Herb Dockter, Scott Grayson, Bruno Benedetti, and Rudy Buckmiller; in front center is Glen "Big Toe" McGill. (McG.)

Lodi Motorcycle Club members pose with an AMA safety banner in the clubhouse on Douglas Avenue (now Golfview Road). Banners went to clubs if all members were accident-free for a year. From left to right are (seated) Dave Buckmiller, Walt Werner (president), chief of police C.S. Jackson, acting mayor W.A. Spooner, and Ezra Ehrhardt (secretary-treasurer); (standing) Roger Janzen (road captain), Don Horstkorta, Al Crete, Rudy Buckmiller (vice president), Herb Dockter, Vernon Meade, Roger Smith, Fran Thoza, Herb Ehrhardt, and Jim Gurney. (SJCHM.)

Stockton Motorcycle Club members assemble around 1940 prior to a road ride. From left to right are Dolly, Johnny, and Glen McGill; Fran Thoza; Dave Buckmiller; Jack Neumeister; four unidentified; Vernon Meade; Walt Werner; Edith and Ezra Ehrhardt; and unidentified. (LMC.)

Modesto Motorcycle Club and Stockton Girls Motorcycle Club members are pictured at a field meet at Oakdale Reservoir (now Woodward Reservoir Regional Park, Stanislaus County) in the 1940s. (S.)

Stockton Motorcycle Club members pose in front of J.F. Donaldson's tire shop, still at 240 North Hunter Street, on Armistice Day (now Veterans Day) 1941. From left to right are (first row) Tim Whyte, Benny Mallo, Max Harr, and Larry Corning; (second row) Vernon Meade, Lester Knapp, Jack Neumeister, Archie Clark, Glen McGill, and Bill Hiles. (H.)

Shown in 1942 romping at Dillon Beach (Marin County) during a Lodi Motorcycle Club road ride are, from left to right, Edith Hamilton, an unidentified child (front), Minnie "Ma" Bloom, Betty Janzen, Ernie Hamilton, Edith Ehrhardt, and Roger Janzen. (LMC.)

The Port Stockton Motorcycle Club was one of the first AMA-sanctioned clubs to allow women members, a few years after its founding as the Vagabonds in 1937. Pictured from left to right are members Ann Gulick, Ruby Alvarez, and Molly Cottrell in the late 1940s. (CA.)

The California Highway Patrol worked with clubs to promote safety, as documented in this late 1940s photograph with the men and women of the Modesto Motorcycle Club. (SMC.)

The Modesto Motorcycle Club hosted a field meet of area club members in about 1946. It was at the clubhouse near Highway 99 and Blue Gum Road (southeast of the current West Campus of Modesto Junior College). The soldier shown was on leave from the 6th Army Light Infantry, stationed in San Francisco. (CA.)

This photograph captures a potato race, the object of which was to pick up potatoes from one's lane and get to the finish line first and with the most potatoes. It was a fun event typical of club field meets. In the background are the Modesto Motorcycle Club's facilities. (CA.)

The Port Stockton Motorcycle Club, originally called the Vagabonds, was founded by workers at the Naval Supply Annex in 1937. Members are pictured here in 1949 in the earliest known group photograph. Included are (first row) Florence "Flossy" Andres, Molly Cottrell, and Ann Gulick; (second row) Shirley Lubin and Eddie Addison; and (third row) Emil Andres, M.C. "Doc" Bacigalupe, Art Noveski, Leonard Andres (third from left), Brad Andres (fourth from left), and August "Sharkey" Alvarez (far right in vest). (CA.)

Tracy Gear Jammers women's auxiliary members are shown looking in American Legion Post 69 at 649 San Benito Street in Hollister (left) and posing with sailors at San Benito and Fifth Streets (right). Both photographs were taken during the infamous July 1947 AMA Gypsy Tour holiday weekend gathering. (WSP.)

This 1946 photograph shows Stockton Motorcycle Club members (from left to right) Jack Neumeister, Roger Nicholson, Joe Genecco, Russell Sykes, and Glen McGill. (SMC).

A Stockton Motorcycle Club award presentation at Glen McGill's (left) dealership honored, from left to right, Myron "Mike" Lubin, Max Harr, and Jan Opperman. (RL.)

Picnics and outdoor activities were enjoyed at club-hosted field meets. Don and Beulah Stover, Stockton Motorcycle Club members, were photographed at a field meet in the late 1940s. (McG.)

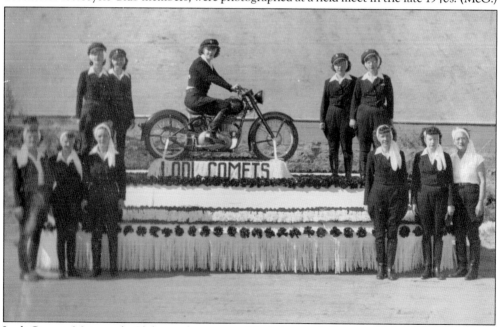

Lodi Comets Motorcycle Club members pose with their parade float in about 1949. From left to right are (first row) Alice Werner, Frieda Connaughton, Edith Hamilton, Dolly McGill, Arta Holbrook, and Minnie "Ma" Bloom; (second row, on the float) Edith Ehrhardt, Bessie Thoza, Pres. Dorothy McGill (on an Indian Arrow motorcycle), Dorothy Smith, and Betty Janzen. (McG.)

The Port Stockton Motorcycle Club is pictured before a parade in about 1950. Participating in local parades gave motorcycle clubs a chance to support their larger communities, promote their hobby, show off their motorcycles, strengthen members' pride and sense of belonging with sharp club uniforms, and demonstrate their values and patriotism with color guards and majorettes. (CA.)

The color guard of the Port Stockton Motorcycle Club is shown in front of the Sears building. (CA.)

Tracy Gear Jammers Motorcycle Club members pose in about 1950. From left to right are (first row) John Elhard, Buck Wooten, Freddy Hunt, Bob Sullivan, and Roy Spangler; (second row) Manuel Silviera, Marshall Skaggs, Rodney Peterman, Bill Blyth, and Tony Souza. (WSP.)

Lodi Comets Motorcycle Club members and their significant others pause during a road ride. From left to right are Cliff Powell, Betty Janzen, unidentified, Ernie Hamilton, Edith Ehrhardt, Roger Janzen, Ezra Ehrhardt, Edith Hamilton, and Alice and Walt Werner. (LMC.)

Lodi Motorcycle Club members participate in a parade in the early 1950s. (RL.)

Members of the Lodi Comets Motorcycle Club pose in 1951 in front of their clubhouse on Golfview Road (south of Micke Grove Regional Park). From left to right are Frieda Connaughton, Rose Pollard, Edith Ehrhardt, Edith Hamilton, Dorothy Smith, Minnie "Ma" Bloom, Frances Lee, Arta Holbrook, Bessie Thoza, Nancy Holbrook, Jean Paoletti, and Dolly McGill. (LMC.)

Members of the Port Stockton Motorcycle Club were photographed during a road ride in the early 1950s. At far left with the cap is Gus Sanguinetti; at center with the white headband is Ann Gulick. (S.)

Lodi Comets Motorcycle Club members are shown in their colors and in formation in 1951, perhaps on Golfview Road. Most are riding Indian motorcycles. (LMC.)

This town in the Sierra foothills gold country was visited by club riders in about 1952. Although the townspeople probably did not appreciate the roar and rumble of this group's takeoff, club members patronized local restaurants and shops and visited historic sites and museums (see page 79). Participants in motorcycle club road rides were usually welcomed, side by side with other tourists. (RL.)

At the Lodi Grape Bowl preparing for a parade in 1952 are Lodi Comets members (from left to right) Nancy Webb, Arta Holbrook, Frances Lee, Mamie ?, Wilma Erideen, Edith Ehrhardt, Beulah Stover, and Minnie "Ma" Bloom. (LMC.)

This 1955 photograph shows a concession stand at a Lodi Motorcycle Club–sponsored race at the Lodi Grape Bowl stadium. From left to right are Audrey Gulick, Bessie Thoza, and Dolly McGill. (McG.)

Members of the Lodi Comets Motorcycle Club pose in 1952. From left to right are (first row) Rose Pollard, Frieda Connaughton, Frances Lee, Nancy Holbrook, and Minnie "Ma" Bloom; (second row) Bessie Thoza, Edith Ehrhardt, Edith Hamilton, Arta Holbrook, Dolly McGill, Jean Paoletti, and Dorothy Smith. (LMC.)

The beauty of the Sierra foothills gold country was captured during this pause in a club road ride to Angels Camp (Calaveras County) in the mid-1950s. (RL.)

This photograph shows a fun blindfold event at a mid-1950s field meet, perhaps at Micke Grove Regional Park between Stockton and Lodi. The motorcycle is a true hybrid—it appears to be a 1940s Harley-Davidson 45ci V-twin military version with 1952–1954 tanks, late 1920s–early 1930s single-fork front end, and a 1950s model K front wheel and fender. (LMC.)

The Port Stockton Motorcycle Club assembled in 1954. Pictured from left to right are (first row) Carl Alvarez, Myron "Mike" Lubin, and Victor Tinkis; (second row) unidentified, Roy Andres, Doug Bacigalupe (below), unidentified, Ruby Alvarez, M.C. "Doc" Bacigalupe, Edith Ehrhardt with AMA trophy, unidentified, Gus Sanguinetti, three unidentified, and August "Sharkey" Alvarez. (LMC.)

Lodi Comets Motorcycle Club members enjoy a skit in their clubhouse. Shown in the mid-1950s are, from left to right, Beulah Stover, Edith Ehrhardt, Arta Holbrook, and Dolly and Glenna McGill. (LMC.)

Leather, denim, and chiffon comfortably blended at motorcycle club dances. The Lodi Motorcycle Club and the Lodi Comets Women's Motorcycle Club got together for annual holiday dinners and dances. Motorcycle clubs also had dances at small resorts in the Sierra Nevada or at venues in the heartland region. (LMC.)

Members of the Golden Bears Motorcycle Club of Manteca are shown in this photograph. (RL.)

Tracy Motorcycle Club members pose showing their colors in July 1965. From left to right are Tom Souza, Tom McNab, Jack Richards, Dick Wittington, Stan White, and Skip Horne. The photograph was taken in the new Cabrillo Park neighborhood, the first major subdivision north of Grant Line Road. (WSP.)

This photograph commemorated the Stockton Motorcycle Club's 70th-anniversary celebration at the Italian Athletic Club in March 1994. Past club presidents shown are, from left to right, Bill Messick (1946), Cecil Rendon (1960–1962), Howard Smith (1965), Jim Newberry (1967–1968, 1974), Gerry Carr (1975–1976), Louie Lagorio (1994), Jim Womack (1966–1967), Chuck Huss (1971), Henry Harvey (1985), Ken Genecco (1983, 1988–1991), Steve Fry (1987), Stewart Barber Sr. (1993), Frank Morris (1979–1980), Fred Kaplan (1984), Bob Berger (1992), and John Jorgensen (1969). Ken Genecco's Vincent C Black Shadow is in front. (SMC.)

Five

FLAT TRACK RACERS, SCRAMBLERS, HILL CLIMBERS, DAREDEVILS, AND MORE

George Schumm poses with his 30.50ci Indian racer in 1913. He was sponsored by the Stockton Motorcycle and Supply Company (see page 16). Motorized bicycles were initially developed around 1905 as "windsplitters" to pace bicycle racers. Soon, the bicycle board-track velodromes were taken over by motorcycle competitions, as were horse tracks and college stadiums. In the following decades, a variety of competitive events evolved: flat oval dirt-track races (short track, half-mile, and mile lengths), hill climbs, drag races, tourist trophy (TT) races, trials competitions, road races, and scrambles, enduros, motocross, and other cross-country or off-road races. (S.)

Otto Walker, from Lathrop (San Joaquin County), was picked in 1914 for the first Harley-Davidson factory racing team (see page 117). In this photograph, he shows his aerodynamic riding position on a Harley-Davidson "banjo" two-cam factory racer at the Beverly Hills Speedway (long board track). (HD.)

This May 1913 photograph shows racers lining up on the mile trotting-horse track at Agricultural Park in Sacramento. The location between Twentieth and Twenty-Third Streets and H and D Streets is now the Boulevard Park historic district/neighborhood. This was the first race for Albert "Shrimp" Burns from Oakdale (Stanislaus County), then 15 years old (perhaps second from right). He finished fourth in the 10-mile feature (see page 118). (CR.)

Stocktonian Robert Franklin Rush is shown on an Excelsior V-twin racer at a mile oval horse track in April 1914. Rush worked for Liberty Cyclery, Bicycles, and Supplies at 205 South California Street in Stockton. (PLC.)

Motorcycle racing roared back after World War I. Pictured here is the original Ascot Park mile oval at South Central and Florence Avenues in Los Angeles on November 30, 1919. Lathrop's Otto Walker (center, third from right) won the 50-mile America's All-Star Sweepstakes race that day. Harley-Davidson professional teammate Shrimp Burns from Oakdale placed second. (HD.)

Members of Harley-Davidson's "Wrecking Crew" team, plus an intruder, pose at old Ascot Park on January 11, 1920. From left to right are Freddie Ludlow, Ralph Hepburn, Oakdale native Albert "Shrimp" Burns, and Lathrop native Otto Walker. Burns had a week earlier switched to the Indian team—hence his smirk at "photobombing" this team photograph, and Walker's apparent embarrassment. (HD.)

Two of the Central Valley's greatest motorcycle racers, Albert Burns (left) and Otto Walker, are pictured after races at old Ascot Park on January 11, 1920. Burns a week earlier had left the Harley-Davidson team to ride for the rival Indian team, reportedly because of tension with Harley team captain Walker. Burns won the 25-mile championship race, and Walker won the 50-mile championship race. (AM.)

Otto Walker is "tucked in" in this iconic photograph of him on the legendary eight-valve Harley-Davidson racer at the one-mile banked board speedway in Fresno. On that track in February 1921, Walker topped 107 miles per hour in the mile time trial, swept every race that day, and won the 50-mile race with an average speed of more than 101 miles per hour—the first 100-plus miles per hour average speed race (see page 117). (HD.)

The Harley-Davidson professional team, known as the Wrecking Crew, poses in 1921. From left to right are Jim Davis, Albert Burns of Oakdale (a former team member who had switched a year prior to Indian), Ray Weishaar, legendary Harley engineer Bill Ottaway, Ralph Hepburn, Fred Ludlow, and Otto Walker of Lathrop. (KM.)

Endurance race winner Finnegan Speer of Sacramento (right) is congratulated by champion and Harley-Davidson dealer/sponsor Dudley Perkins in the 1920s. Lengthy endurance races were common in the 1910s–1920s, usually based on number of laps or distance completed in a set time. (KM.)

Timed hill climb competitions, "vertical drag races," were very popular in the 1920s and 1930s. Spectators flocked to the base and flanks of the hill. This photograph captured the start of a 1922 hill climb run in the Tracy Hills, southwest of Tracy in San Joaquin County. (RV.)

Hill climb great Dudley Perkins, assisted by Pat Speer, prepares to launch his specialized Harley-Davidson in the 1920s. Note the rear tire chains for added traction. Perkins began his career in Stockton (see pages 13 and 119). (KM.)

Dudley Perkins on a Harley-Davidson won the 1928 National Hill Climb on what is now called "Motorcycle Hill" in the Oakland Hills (east of current Julian Court in El Cerrito), overlooking San Pablo Bay. (KM.)

"Speedway" became the name for races on a short oval flat track using powerful, light motorcycles with no brakes. The speedway race lineup shown here was at Sacramento Stadium (now Hughes Stadium, near Sutterville Road) at Sacramento Junior College in the early 1930s. Leonard Andres of Stockton is the fourth rider from the right on a British JAP-powered motorcycle (see page 120). These Friday night races were among the most popular spectator events in the Valley. (KM.)

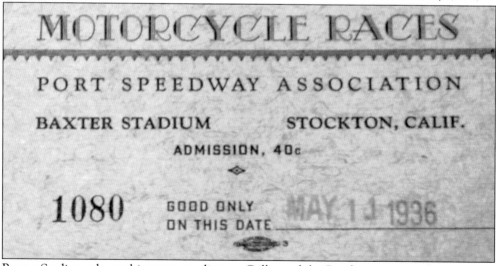

Baxter Stadium, the multipurpose stadium at College of the Pacific, was a popular venue for motorcycle races. The stadium was also where Amos Alonzo Stagg coached football from 1933 to 1946, where All-American football player Eddie LeBaron and other legends played, and where the 1949 College of the Pacific Tigers went 11-0, set an NCAA scoring record, and earned a No. 10 national ranking. (SMC.)

The mile oval horse track at the San Joaquin County Fairgrounds on South Airport Way in Stockton was an important motorcycle racing venue. The track hosted oval and tourist trophy races, dirt track races with at least one right turn and jump. Armando Magri of Sacramento is shown here on his Harley-Davidson before a TT race at the fairgrounds in about 1939. (KM.)

Pictured in the pits are TT racers (from left to right) Dick "Jughead" Milligan (6) of Glendale, Sam Arena of Watsonville/San Jose (79, in back), and Jack Cottrell (21) of San Francisco. The photograph was taken by Armando Magri (2) of Sacramento. (KM.)

Glen McGill of Stockton is shown competing in an Ospital Canyon hill climb southwest of Vernalis, near the San Joaquin–Stanislaus County line, in about 1940. The event was promoted by the Modesto Motorcycle Club. (DK.)

This ticket was to a hill climb competition in Ospital Canyon, now called Hospital Creek. The location, not to be confused with the modern Carnegie State Vehicular Recreation Area on Corral Hollow Road, is southwest of Westley; the ticket incorrectly reads southeast. The event was sponsored by the California Highway Patrol and promoted by the Modesto Motorcycle Club. (DK.)

ADMIT ONE
Modesto Motor Cycle Hill Climb
Five Miles Southeast of Westley
⟵————— Follow the Arrows ⟶—————⟶
1 p.m. April 25 ❖ Rain Date May 2
PROFESSIONAL HILL CLIMBERS
ADMISSION 40c
Promoted by the Modesto Motor Cycle Club
Official A. M. A. No. 86
Management Not Responsible for Accidents

This photograph shows a Class C short track race at Lodi Stadium (now the Grape Bowl at 221 Lawrence Avenue), a New Deal WPA project still under construction in the late 1930s. From left to right are riders Tom Turner (97), Sam Hicks (17), Bob Chaves (20), Wayne Bias (21), Charlie West (31), and Aldo "Al" Scoffone (96). Class C was started in 1934 during the Great Depression to encourage amateur racers with largely stock motorcycles. It was called "run what you brung" because most racers rode their bikes to the track. (DK.)

Another Class C short track race at Lodi Stadium featured, from left to right, unidentified (55), Bob Chaves (20) of San Jose, unidentified (56), unidentified (3), Sam Hicks (17), Armando Magri (2) of Sacramento, and Tom Turner (97). (KM.)

Ed "Iron Man" Kretz Sr. of Pomona leads a scrambles (off-road) race in William Micke's oak grove, between Lodi and Stockton (now Micke Grove Regional Park), in this photograph from about 1940. Kretz was a dominant racer in the 1930s–1940s, won the first Daytona 200, and is an AMA Hall of Fame honoree. (DK.)

Sam Arena of Watsonville/San Jose is pictured topping the hill and getting the checkered flag in a 1930s Oakland Hills (El Cerrito) hill climb. Arena is in the AMA Hall of Fame. (DK.)

Glen McGill (right) is shown after winning the 1950 "Turkey Trot" Thanksgiving Scrambles race, sponsored by the Port Stockton Motorcycle Club. McGill won on a flat rear tire, so a special oval trophy was made and presented to him. (McG.)

Harold Ott receives a race trophy at Lodi Stadium around 1950. From left to right are Roy Murray on a 500cc Matchless single, two unidentified, Harold "Huck" Ott on a 1949 square-barrel 500cc Triumph, Glen McGill, and Ray Weser, the AMA NorCal district service representative. (R.P.)

The 1952 Stockton Mile (flat track) race at the San Joaquin County Fairgrounds was sponsored by the Stockton Motorcycle Club. Pictured at the start/finish line are, from left to right, racers Wally Cox (105) of Raisin City, Russell Johnson (182) of San Jose, and Fred Quinn (152) of Oakland. (S.)

Don "Coley" Coleman of Stockton and an unidentified "trophy girl" pose to promote the June 17, 1951, Stockton Mile (flat track) race at the San Joaquin County Fairgrounds. (C.)

Pete Duke of Tulare is "crossed up" on a 1951 Harley-Davidson WR at the Stockton Mile (flat track) race in 1953. (S.)

Hugging the rail during the 1952 Stockton Mile are, from left to right, Warren Thieman (145y) of San Francisco, Bob Speith (44y) of North Sacramento, and unidentified (61z). (S.)

Motorcycle daredevils teeter above Stockton's Weber Avenue at Hunter Square in October 1953. The cable spanned the 1910 Hotel Stockton and the San Joaquin County Courthouse (right), which was built in 1890–1891 and razed in 1961. (BOS.)

In the early 1950s, an American quarter horse challenges a motorcycle—only one is bucking. This was typical "halftime" entertainment by the Shelby Stables at the Fort Sutter Flat Track. (RL.)

Joe Leonard of San Jose won the 1953 Stockton Mile (flat track) race at the San Joaquin County Fairgrounds on a Harley-Davidson KR. Leonard won the AMA Grand National series in 1954, 1956, and 1957, and the Daytona 200 Road Race in 1957 and 1958 before focusing on USAC automobile racing in the 1960s. He is in the AMA Hall of Fame. (S.)

This is the only known photograph of Joe Leonard competing in a hill climb. This competition was in Ospital Canyon, now called Hospital Creek (see page 92), in the hills east of San Jose, where Leonard lived. He was a member of the San Jose Motorcycle Club, known as "the Dons." (RL.)

Stocktonians Leonard Andres (left) and his son Brad are both AMA Hall of Fame honorees (see pages 120 and 121). Brad won three Daytona 200s and was the dominant road racer in the 1950s. Leonard, too, was a champion racer, a member of the Vagabonds/Port Stockton Motorcycle Club (see chapter four), and a master engine builder. The family had Harley-Davidson dealerships in Modesto, Stockton, and San Diego (see pages 20–21). They posed for this photograph in 1953. (RL.)

Trials is a non-timed motorcycle competition in which riders navigate an off-road obstacle course and lose points for putting their feet down or stalling. This photograph is of Don "Coley" Coleman at a trials meet at Lodi Cycle Bowl, at 5801 East Morse Road, in 1954. (C.)

John "Jorgy" Jorgensen of
Stockton (right) and "Icky"
Stover of Stockton (below) on a
Triumph 500cc twin are shown
at a 1954 trials competition
at Lodi Cycle Bowl. (S.)

A trials course was developed by the Stockton Motorcycle Club near the Calaveras River and the Wilson Way bridge. An unidentified rider is shown on the course in 1954. (RL.)

Richard Fern of Stockton negotiates a water hazard on the Stockton Motorcycle Club's trials course. (RL.)

Kenny Eggers of Arnold (Calaveras County) is shown winning the first AMA road race in the western United States at Willow Springs International Raceway in Rosamond, Kern County, California, in 1954. Eggers was riding one of four BSA A7 Shooting Star 500cc twins shipped from England for the famous race at Daytona, Florida, where BSA took the first five places. Eggers has been inducted into the AMA Hall of Fame. (S.)

Lodi Cycle Bowl, at 5801 East Morse Road, was developed by the Lodi Motorcycle Club beginning in 1953. This photograph shows the short track/TT venue about a year after work started. It has come a long way since then. (S.)

Brad Andres, on a Harley-Davidson KR, is shown winning the 1955 Stockton Mile (flat track) race at the San Joaquin County Fairgrounds. This was the year he turned pro and won his first Daytona 200 (see page 121). (S.)

A drag race covers a straight quarter mile from a standing start. Motorcycles competed along with "hot rod" street cars and specialized dragsters. This photograph shows Karl Ross of Stockton, a drag race winner, around 1954. Ross and Mike Buckenham modified this 1952 Triumph 650cc Thunderbird as a drag bike. (MB.)

Muddy fields near Linden, east of Stockton, provided challenges for this female enduro competitor in the early 1950s. This may have been a timekeeping enduro, the object of which was for competitors to arrive at pre-defined checkpoints according to a strict schedule. Most modern US enduro events are lengthy offroad "rallies" in which racers compete to reach the end of each of multiple sections or laps in the fastest time. (McG.)

A motorcycle daredevil show provided thrilling entertainment at the 1955 San Joaquin County Fair in Stockton. (BOS.)

Starter Don "Smokey" Stover of Stockton (second from left) directs rider Troy "Pete" Rupe of Stockton at Lodi Cycle Bowl in the mid-1950s. (S.)

The three riders in this 1955 scrambles race at Lodi Cycle Bowl wearing polka-dot jerseys were members of the Polka Dots Motorcycle Club from Sacramento/Rancho Cordova. (S.)

The AMA District 36 or Valley Council 1955 season high-points winners assembled in Modesto. From left to right are (first row) Hank Hergenroder, Bob Matia, unidentified, and Vern Carock; (second row) Harold Hergenroder, Tom Howard (overall high-points winner), unidentified, Don "Coley" Coleman, and Glen McGill. (TH.)

Lodi Cycle Bowl scrambles race winners pose in 1956. From left to right are Frank Marinovich (69) of Fairfield on a 650cc Triumph, trophy girl Rose Pollard, Troy "Pete" Rupe of Stockton on a 1956 Triumph TR6, and Don "Coley" Coleman of Stockton on a BSA Gold Star. (TH.)

John McGill of Stockton is shown on a Triumph exiting turn two at Lodi Cycle Bowl in 1959. John literally grew up as a member of the motorcycling community (see page 66) and in his parents' motorcycle dealerships (see page 23). As a young adult, he ran the shop in Stockton and amazed customers by not only knowing where every part was on the shelves, but also reciting part numbers by heart. He was a great joke and storyteller, and he sponsored many young racers, paying their entry fees and loaning or giving them motorcycles on which to learn. (McG.)

The incident captured here adds a touch of *On Any Sunday*–style humor. It was not Mike Buckenham's greatest moment, but he was a local legend racer and street rider. He seldom "got off," but in this case, he said he was stubborn and wanted to stay with the bike. (MB.)

Tom Howard of Stockton (145, on right) is pictured at the flight start of the 100-mile Catalina Island Invitational Grand Prix Road Race in 1958. Howard was invited to compete in 1956, 1957, and this final race in 1958. The annual road race was started in 1950 and was patterned after the historic Isle of Mann races. (TH).

Tom Howard was pushing hard on the last lap of the Catalina Grand Prix and his friend, actor Lee Marvin, was watching behind the bales (center). Howard insists he did not "lay the bike down." (TH.)

Tom Howard entered the Pro ranks in 1960. This photograph shows him on his 500cc Triumph at Lodi Cycle Bowl. (TH.)

Stockton racer Nick Fletcher poses on his 250cc BSA in 1960 at the Lodi Cycle Bowl. Fletcher was a well-liked and respected rider. He had raced for six years and was one of the Valley's outstanding amateur racers. Unfortunately, he died in a motorcycle accident shortly after this photograph was taken, at 22 years of age. (J.)

Trophy winners assemble after evening races at Lodi Cycle Bowl in 1960. The winners were, from left to right, Arnold Castelhano (30c), Butch Corder (92c), Roger McCarthy (57r), Cliff "Bud" Aksland (70a), Ray Huff (58a), unidentified (58g), Tom Howard (1j), and John "Jorgy" Jorgensen (38z). (RL.)

Cecil Rendon II of Stockton was for many years the track announcer for Stockton Motorcycle Club events. He is shown on a little 50cc Tohatsu at Lodi Cycle Bowl, although he usually raced a 200cc Triumph Tiger Cub. He owned Stattui's Saddles, announced rodeos throughout the West Coast, was a musician and stringed instrument repairer, and served three terms as president of the Stockton Motorcycle Club. (R.)

Tom Howard (left) and John Jorgensen are shown dueling at Lodi Cycle Bowl in about 1960. Is Howard making an inside pass or is Jorgy making an outside pass? It depends on who is asked. (TH.)

Tracy's Jimmy Odom was a Northern California flat track star in the 1960s–1970s, a solid road racer (fifth at Daytona in 1971), and set a motorcycle land speed record of 336 miles per hour at Bonneville. He also survived a crash at 289 miles per hour, the highest speed survival at the time. He has been inducted into the Hot Shoe Hall of Fame, established in 2020 to recognize flat track and speedway standouts. (JO.)

Saturday evening short track racing at Modesto's "playland" was popular in 1965. Riders shown include Ray Huff (69y) in the foreground; from left to right are (first row) Jim Monegan (33e), Leon Bradford (82e), and "Stinky" Sargenti (59) (the others are unidentified); (second row) Chuck Huss (23e), Davie Clark (65z), Dick Blank (120y), Jim Frakes (111z), and Bob White (30y) (the others are unidentified). Highway 99 and the Grange (feed) Company are in the background behind the track. (S.)

Richard Hardmeyer (59y) of Herald (southern Sacramento County) was photographed on his 650cc Triumph leading this 1964 TT race at the Placer County Speedway in Roseville. (RH.)

Kenny Roberts Sr. of Modesto (upper left) celebrates a short track victory in 1970. From left to right are (first row) mechanic Fred Moberg, Cliff "Bud" Aksland of Manteca, and Terry Sage of Stockton; (second row) Roberts and Skip Aksland of Manteca. In the mid-1960s, Roberts began competing at informal tracks, such as "playland" in Modesto (see page 113) and "Simpson-Lee" in the Stanislaus River bottomlands of Ripon, riding Tohatsu and Hodaka dirt bikes. His racing career really started in 1968, when Manteca Suzuki dealer Bud Aksland sponsored him. Roberts became one of the greatest motorcycle racers of all time. He won the AMA National Championships in 1973, 1974, and 1977 and FIM World Championships in 1978, 1979, and 1980 (see page 123). (S.)

Master machinist Ron Myer of Harold began building drag motorcycles in the 1960s at age 12. He went on to hold many national and track records at dragstrips such as Fremont (Baylands Raceway) and Sacramento Raceway (6.68 seconds elapsed time, 198 miles per hour top speed). Now in his 70s, Myer continues to race and win at Sacramento, recently covering the quarter mile in a 7.24-second, 184 miles per hour pass. (RM.)

Six

AMA HALL OF FAME HONOREES

The American Motorcyclist Association supports all motorcyclists in the United States and is the largest member-driven motorcycling organization in the world. It sprang from two preceding associations. The Federation of American Motorcyclists (FAM) was established in 1903 to "promote the general interests of motorcycling; to . . . protect the rights of motorcyclists; to facilitate touring; to assist in the good roads movement; and to . . . assist in the regulation of motorcycle racing and other competition." The Motorcycle and Allied Trades Association (MATA) formed in 1916 and picked up the mission of FAM when FAM ceased operating in 1919. MATA registered riders and clubs, sanctioned national racing championships, and supported Gypsy Tour gatherings. The MATA Education and Competition Committee became the American Motorcycle Association in 1924, and in 1976, its name was changed to the American Motorcyclist Association. A separate nonprofit, the American Motorcycle Heritage Foundation, was formed in 1982 to create a museum in collaboration with the Antique Motorcycle Club of America. The current AMA Motorcycle Hall of Fame Museum in Pickerington, Ohio, opened in 1999. The 11 AMA Hall of Fame honorees profiled in this chapter were all associated with the northern San Joaquin Valley. (AMA.)

George Wyman was born in Oakland and died in Stockton. In 1903, he was the first motorcyclist to ride from coast to coast. As a teen, Wyman caught the bicycling bug of the 1880s–1890s. He became a leading bicycle racer and in 1900 went to Australia to compete. Foreshadowing his transcontinental ride, he was among the first to bicycle the full perimeter of the Australian continent. On May 16, 1903, Wyman began his ride across the United States in a three-piece wool suit, shirt and tie, and cap. He was astride a 1.25-horsepower motorcycle, a 1902 California. The launch point in San Francisco was called Newspaper Square, but the local press expressed little excitement. Wyman himself described and photographed the adventure for the first magazine devoted to motorcycling, *The Motorcycle Magazine.* Roadways were limited and often impassable; Wyman often had to ride across the ties of railroad tracks, as he did through the train snowsheds crossing the Sierra Nevada. He frequently had to assist the feeble motorcycle by pedaling or dismounting and pushing. He made many "bailing wire" roadside repairs and had difficulty finding gasoline and oil. At Albany, New York, he gave up on repairs and pedaled the final 150 miles to New York City. (GWMP.)

OTTO WALKER ON HARLEY-DAVIDSON EIGHT VALVE MACHINE WHICH AVERAGED 104.43 M. P. H. IN 25 MILE RACE AT BEVERLY, CALIFORNIA, APRIL 24, 1921

Otto Walker was a leading racer in the 1910s and early 1920s and was one of the first factory riders for Harley-Davidson. He was the first to win a race with an average speed of more than 100 miles per hour. Harry Otto Walker was born in Lathrop (San Joaquin County) in 1890. By 1913, he was the top amateur racer on the West Coast, winning at fairgrounds, dirt ovals, and board tracks. In 1915, he won Harley-Davidson's first national victory, a 300-mile road race in Venice, California. That July, he won the most prestigious race in America, the Dodge City 300 on the two-mile dirt oval. After World War I, in 1920, Walker won the national championship on the two-mile board track at Sheepshead Bay Speedway in Brooklyn; the 50- and 100-mile nationals at old Ascot Park in Los Angeles (see pages 85–87); and the 100-mile championship in Marion, Indiana. In 1921, on the mile board track in Fresno, Walker won the 50-mile race with an average speed of more than 101 miles per hour; he also won the 1-, 10-, and 15-mile races (see page 87). In 1922, on the board track in Beverly Hills, he broke six American speed records (see page 84). Harley-Davidson shut down its racing program after the 1922 season. Walker retired from racing and ran a sport-fishing service on the Sacramento River. (HD.)

Albert "Shrimp" Burns was born in Oakdale (Stanislaus County) in 1898. In 1913, he entered his first race, on the trotting track at Agricultural Park in Sacramento (see page 84), and finished fourth in the 10-mile feature. Experienced racers including Otto Walker kept the 15-year-old newcomer out of most other Northern California races. He was, however, allowed to compete at San Jose and earned his first win—the youngest champion of his era. After World War I, in 1919, the 20-year-old Shrimp won at Fresno Speedway and was signed by Harley-Davidson to his first factory contract. That summer, he won races throughout the East Coast and the Midwest. He won the final major race of the 1919 season, a 100-mile national championship on the two-mile board track at Sheepshead Bay Speedway in Brooklyn. Burns surprisingly switched to the rival Indian team for the 1920 season, probably because he harbored resentment toward Harley team captain Walker (see pages 85–87). He soon won the 25-mile national at old Ascot Park in Los Angeles. Burns also won the 1921 opener on the 1.25-mile board speedway in Beverly Hills. Tragically, he died later that year on the track in Toledo, Ohio, at the Fort Miami Mile race. (AMA.)

The AMA named its most prestigious award for Dudley Perkins and first presented it to him. Perkins was a legendary figure in the first century of US motorcycling: a hill climb champion, a Harley-Davidson dealer, and a racing team sponsor and manager. He was born in 1893 in Kern County and spent his childhood in Stockton. In 1911, he got a job at Land & Dorr Motorcycles in Stockton (see page 13) and soon began competing in local races. In 1913, Perkins purchased a DeLuxe and Jefferson dealership and soon added Harley-Davidson—in 2014, Dudley Perkins Harley-Davidson of South San Francisco celebrated its 100th anniversary. Perkins began competing in hill climbs in 1915, eventually winning 12 California hill climb championships (see page 89). One of the biggest competitive motorcycling events in the 1910s and early 1920s was the National Hill Climb on Capistrano Hill in Santa Ana, which drew 20,000–30,000 spectators each year. In 1920, Perkins was the first in six years to conquer the hill. He competed in hill climbs into 1943, at 50 years of age. In the 1930s, Perkins joined the new AMA Competition Committee and became its longest-serving member. He sponsored many AMA racing events, notably the San Jose Mile, and many riders, including Mark Brelsford and Mert Lawill, both of whom won national championships. (KM.)

Leonard Andres was a well-known motorcycle racer in the 1930s (shown here in about 1935), a respected tuner in the 1950s–1960s, and a successful motorcycle dealer from the 1940s to the 1970s. Andres was born in Eureka, Humboldt County, California, and raised in Stockton. He and his brothers Gene and Roy initially raced on larger Northern California dirt tracks, but Leonard started focusing on speedway racing, winning numerous Class A short track victories in the early 1930s on lightweight British JAP-powered speedway bikes (see page 90). In the mid-1930s, he began racing a 45ci Harley-Davidson, winning in 1937 the first Pacific Coast TT Championship in Hollister, San Benito County, California. Andres retired from serious racing in 1938 after opening a Harley-Davidson dealership in Modesto (see pages 20–21). He later opened dealerships in Stockton and San Diego. In the 1950s, his son Brad started his own hall-of-fame racing career with his dad as an engine builder and tuner (see page 100). Leonard's engine-building services were in heavy demand by top riders of the era. He continued to build racing engines after Brad retired from racing, and he served on the AMA Competition Committee. (KM.)

Brad Andres was born in Stockton and started riding at age five. He was the only rider to win the AMA Grand National Championship in his rookie year, as well as to win the first and last races of his AMA career. He was the greatest road racer in the mid-to-late 1950s; of his 12 AMA wins, 10 were on road courses, and he won three Daytona 200s. The Andres family moved to San Diego when Brad was 16, and he soon was winning at Southern California tracks. In 1955, he won his first professional race, the famous Daytona (Florida) 200, riding a Harley-Davidson tuned by his father (see pages 100 and 104); Brad was 19, the youngest rider to win Daytona. He won Daytona again in 1959 and 1960, tying the record for wins and becoming the last winner on the beach. In 1956, an accident at Ascot Park killed Andres's friend Chuck Basney and severely injured Brad. After a year to heal, he came back in 1958 and continued winning into 1960. After his third Daytona win, Andres retired to manage the family motorcycle dealership. Harley-Davidson asked him to come out of retirement for one more race, and he won the 150-mile road race at Watkins Glen, New York, the final race of his career. (HD.)

Alex "Jorgy" Jorgensen of Stockton is one of the few AMA Grand National riders to have won in all four dirt-track disciplines: short track, TT, half mile, and mile. He is the only racer to have achieved that feat in his first four Grand National wins. He also competed on four different motorcycle brands for his Grand National wins: Can-Am, BSA, Norton, and Harley-Davidson. Jorgy began his racing career at Lodi Cycle Bowl in the late 1960s. He said that "racing at Lodi helped me to become a very versatile racer. I was able to compete in several different classes ranging from 100cc to . . . 650cc bikes and with both short track and TT events. I was fortunate to experiment with different brands, geometries, etc." Jorgensen was the last rider to win AMA Grand National races on Norton and BSA motorcycles—both wins at Ascot Park in Gardena, Los Angeles County. On the other hand, he won the first Grand National race on a Can-Am motorcycle. He also had the first Grand National victory with the Rotax four-stroke single engine, a TT race at Ascot. With Gary Scott, Jorgensen holds the record for the most AMA Grand National wins at Ascot Park: six. (AJ.)

Modesto native Kenny Roberts Sr. first focused on motorcycle racing in 1968, sponsored by Bud Aksland from Manteca. By 1970, Roberts was a regular winner at Lodi Cycle Bowl and other dirt tracks in the Valley and Bay Area (see page 114) and he signed with Yamaha. As a rookie in 1972, he won the Grand National race in the Houston Astrodome. He went on to win the 1973 and 1974 Grand National championships. He won 47 AMA nationals in all the major disciplines of the era: short track, TT, half mile, mile, and road racing. He won the prestigious Daytona 200 three times. He was named AMA Pro Athlete of the Year three times: 1973, 1974, and 1979. In 1977, Roberts won six of the seven AMA road races and the national championship. In 1978, he went overseas for the Federation Internationale Motorcyliste (FIM) World 500cc Grand Prix Road Racing series. Roberts became the first American to win a world title. He won three consecutive world championships, in 1978, 1979, and 1980. "King" Kenny retired from racing after the 1983 season and formed his own team, which won multiple championships in the early 1990s. In the late 1990s, he focused on engine development. In 1998, Roberts was presented a special AMA Lifetime Achievement Award. (AMA.)

Stocktonian Fred Merkel was a three-time AMA Superbike champion and went overseas and won two Superbike world championships. "Flying" Fred began his racing career at Lodi Cycle Bowl and other dirt tracks in California. In 1981, he began riding 250cc road racing motorcycles and was the AMA Novice Rider of the Year. He turned pro the following year, and in 1983 was hired by Honda to race AMA Superbikes. Merkel finished his 1983 rookie season in third place and began a string of 20 AMA Superbike wins, the most by any rider at that time. In 1984, he not only won the AMA Superbike title, but he did so by winning a record 10 AMA Superbike races. The FIM World Superbike Championships were initiated in 1988, and Merkel won the premier season. He won again in 1989. Merkel returned to the United States in 1994 and won one race on a Kawasaki and seven races for Suzuki, moving him to second place in AMA 750 SuperSport career wins. Merkel retired from racing after the 1995 season and moved with his family to New Zealand. (AMA.)

Longtime Modesto resident Jimmy Filice was the AMA Flat Track Rookie of the Year in 1981. He later dominated AMA 250cc Grand Prix Road Racing, winning a total of 29 AMA national races. In his 1981 rookie expert season, Filice joined the Roberts/Lawwill team, excelled on the dirt, and began having success on paved road courses, winning the 250 Grand Prix at Pocono, Pennsylvania. In the mid-to-late 1980s, Filice raced AMA Superbikes, but his bikes were not competitive. Filice almost returned full-time to dirt tracks, but in 1988, he was asked to ride at the 250 Grand Prix at Laguna Seca (Monterey County) and won convincingly. In 1991, Filice won the AMA 250 Grand Prix title, his first professional championship a full decade into his pro career. Filice dominated the 1993 AMA 250 Grand Prix series, winning nine of 10 rounds on his way to his second championship. He focused on racing in Europe for a few years, but also won several AMA Grand Prix races, including the Daytona road race in 1994. He ran the Kenny Roberts Training Camp in Barcelona, Spain, for several years, then in 2001, raced a full AMA 250 Grand Prix season for the first time since 1993 and won his third national title. (AMA.)

Chris Carr was born in Stockton and began racing at the nearby Lodi Cycle Bowl in 1973 when he was six—his parents were active members of the Lodi Motorcycle Club, and Chris literally grew up at the track, idolizing Kenny Roberts and Alex Jorgensen. Carr turned pro in 1985 and was named AMA Flat Track Rookie of the Year. In 1989, he became a Harley-Davidson team rider and for a few years had epic battles with teammate Scott Parker. Carr won the Grand National championship in 1992, with national wins including mile, half-mile, short track, and TT events. In 1995, he focused on competing in the AMA Superbike Road Racing series and was named AMA Superbike Rookie of the Year. Carr again focused on Grand National racing in 2001 and won the AMA Grand National Championship in 2001, 2002, 2003, 2004, and 2005—giving him a total of seven Grand National Championships and the second-most career wins in AMA Grand National history. Carr was named AMA Pro Athlete of the Year in 2003. In 2006, at the Bonneville Salt Flats, he became the fastest motorcycle rider in the world and the first to exceed 350 miles per hour. (AMA.)

INDEX

DISCOVER THOUSANDS OF LOCAL HISTORY BOOKS FEATURING MILLIONS OF VINTAGE IMAGES

Arcadia Publishing, the leading local history publisher in the United States, is committed to making history accessible and meaningful through publishing books that celebrate and preserve the heritage of America's people and places.

Find more books like this at
www.arcadiapublishing.com

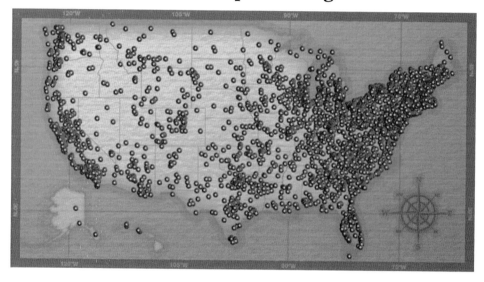

Search for your hometown history, your old stomping grounds, and even your favorite sports team.

Consistent with our mission to preserve history on a local level, this book was printed in South Carolina on American-made paper and manufactured entirely in the United States. Products carrying the accredited Forest Stewardship Council (FSC) label are printed on 100 percent FSC-certified paper.

MADE IN THE